MOMMY MEANS BUSINESS

How To Maximize Your Earning Potential While Running Your Household

Anna Santos

10-10-10
Publishing

MOMMY MEANS BUSINESS
How To Maximize Your Earning Potential While Running Your Household

www.annasantoshub.com

Copyright © 2018 by ANNA SANTOS
ISBN: 978-1-77277-213-5

Publisher
10-10-10 Publishing
Markham, ON
Canada

Printed in Canada and the United States of America

TABLE OF CONTENTS

DEDICATION

I dedicate this book in honour of
my late grandmothers in heaven:
Puring Rivera & **Gloria Vasquez**

I also dedicate this book to all parents around the world.

FOREWORD

This book is one obvious proof that moms are really, really fantastic. I can't imagine how this world that we live in would be like without moms around.

I've known Anna as a very passionate person, and she believes that one of the noblest ways to serve God is through our families. She also knows that every mom has this special gift to show compassion and empathy with a deep-rooted desire to help others who are in the same situation like herself before coming up with a very great decision.

She wrote this book because she feels every mom's heart. As the saying goes, "It takes one to know one." But even if you're not a mom, she also intends to share her message to you regardless.

To all moms and dads who felt stuck, I highly recommend reading this book. You'll very much learn from her own experiences and expertise that it is really possible to enjoy both worlds of being a parent and an entrepreneur at the same time in the very comfort of your own home!

Mommy Means Business© is a game changer. And she nailed it.

Hats off to you, Anna! I don't know where that courage came from. But this is what I know. You're a mom, and everything says it all.

Raymond Aaron
New York Times Bestselling Author

ACKNOWLEDGMENTS

I would like to gladly express my sincere gratitude to all those who gave me, and continue to provide me with, such a tremendous amount of inspiration and support in every way possible to help me grow in all aspects of my wellbeing.

I deeply thank my **Creator** who always directs me and answers my prayers. Thank you, Lord, for providing me with strength, courage, and wisdom to get to where I am now. I praise and thank you, my God, my Lord, and my Savior.

I am very thankful to the most special person in my life, my husband, **Christopher Santos**, for letting me spread my wings and for supporting me in my every endeavor. Thank you for believing that I can do great things beyond my imagination. Most of all, thank you for making me the most privileged woman in the universe to earn the title, "Mrs. Santos." I really can't thank you enough for your love and understanding despite my countless flaws as a person, a mom, and, of course, a wife. You're God's greatest gift to me. I love you, Hon!

To my precious treasures, my four kids: **Sophia Margarette**, my artist daughter; **Danver Jude**, my musically inclined and talented son; **Santino Miguel**, my engineer-in-the-making son; and **Christiann Mikhail**, my miracle boy. Mom loves you all so much.

How can I not thank these two people, my parents, who brought me into the world: **Nanay Yolly** and **Tatay Ver.** Thank you for being so selfless in taking care of my family all this time. I love you both so much. To my brothers, **Michael Vasquez** and **Marco Vasquez**, thank you. I also thank **Rebecca Ocampo** (Dada) for being the best nanny in the world. Also, thank you to my dear **in-laws** and **relatives.**

Thank you to my parish, **St. Therese of the Child Jesus**, for instilling in me that kind of faith in God since I was in Grade 2. A special mention to **Fr. Noel V. Abutal,** for making our parish church astoundingly beautiful! Thanks, Padre!

I also thank my charismatic community, **The Loved Flock**, for honing my personal relationship with God. To **Bro. Vincent "Bingbong" Crisologo,** our founder; **Bro. Jing Mendoza,** our spiritual counselor; and **Rev. Msgr. Albert Venus**, our spiritual director. You have no idea what a huge difference you made in my life's spiritual journey. Also, a million thanks to my personal spiritual counselor, **Bro. Don Quilao**, for your generosity with your time and wisdom. A special thank you, **Deacon Bob Rosales,** for your unwavering support to our community. You're a rock star! Also, special thanks to Tita **Minerva Hilado Garcia,** who has been very supportive to me, in that her words of encouragement kept me going.

Thank you, **Sta. Teresita Central School,** where I attended my elementary education. I also thank my academic adviser in high school, **Sir Max Muldong**, from **La Consolacion College,** in Manila. To my university dean, **Madam Charito Bermido**, thank you for your kind and encouraging words. And to my entire **Centro Escolar University family**, thank you! Thank you, **Mrs. MaryAnne Rekuta** and **Madam Tiffany Cancian** of St. James Catholic School, my sons' teachers.

To my only few trusted friends, thank you: **Sheilah Mesina, Doreyn Sucgang, Roxan delos Santos, Juvy Malayba, Hazel Tiratira, Mildred Convento,** and **Liza Consolacion.** Thank you to my new friends, **Joyce Sosoban-Roa** and **Crestine Carson.** Also, many thanks to my local business partners, **Melissa** and **Leo Domingo,** and **Dori Romero**.

I'm also thankful to my **Real Estate Investing Network** (REIN) family in Toronto, Canada, especially to my mentors **Richard Dolan, Patrick Francey, Don R. Campbell**, and **Peter Kinch**. Thank you to my real estate investing team: **Hugo Dos Reis** from the Vine Group; **Eva Kotsopoulos**, my real estate agent from RE/MAX and, of course, to my **accountant** and **real estate lawyers**, thank you.

I'd also like to thank this very young and inspiring couple, **Eduard** and **Akie Reformina**. A million thanks to my **Fast Track Academy family.** You rock!

Thank you, **Golden Balangay Awards for Filipino-Canadian Achievers** and **Kubo Magazine,** for nominating me in the *Young Entrepreneur of the Year* category, in 2017. I admire your mission to recognize our tribe's contribution to the Canadian society. I also am honored to personally know Tita **Cora Cristobal**, of the Toronto Women's Club, Ltd. I'm also inspired by the Financial Literacy channel,

ANC OnTheMoney, hosted by **Salve Duplito** and **Edric Mendoza**.

Thank you to my virtual business mentors: **Dean Pax Lapid, Paulo Tibig, Noel Jorge Wieneke, Rex Mendoza, Francis Kong,** and **Sir Edward Lee**.

My long-time inspiration as a woman and as an entrepreneur, Socorro Ramos, or simply known as **Nanay Coring**, founder and pillar of the National Book Store, built in the 1940s. You've just proven to me that a woman has everything it takes to succeed and that age is only a number.

My special thanks to my **St. Michael's Hospital** family in Toronto. Thank you for believing in me and being my best employer ever! St. Michael, you'll always be my urban angel. To my friends and ex-colleagues, **Nancy Mesa** and **Hailey Garcia-Gonzalez,** thank you so much for being part of my life.

Of course, to a friend and a business client, **Dr. Scott Kapoor**. Thank you, Scott, for opening doors of opportunities for me.

Thank you to the crew and staff of **Truly Rich Club's SuccessLive** segment, where I globally appeared online for a business-related interview with Bro. Bo Sanchez. Thank you so much **Marco Victoria, Cecille Leano Sia, Laurent Dionisio, Niko Bolante, Mai Aberilla Neri, Ian Quiazon,** Tita **Pinkie Victoria,** and Tita **Chelle Crisanto**.

Last but not least, my whole list of gratitude can never be complete without having to thank infinitely, the founder of my very favorite club in my lifetime, **Bro. Bo Sanchez,** of the Truly Rich Club. I'll never get tired of thanking you, as it changed me a whole lot to a substantial degree of greatness, abundance, and purpose because of your wisdom and teachings. Bro. Bo, you're the best!

And to all of you, my readers, I thank you for grabbing this book, especially to all the parents around the world. From my heart, I salute all of you. Kudos for a job well done!

Continue to be blessed, and be a blessing to others.

Anna Santos
Mommy Means Business©
Author & Speaker
Entrepreneur

INTRODUCTION
St. Francis of Assisi

"Start by doing what's necessary; then do what's possible;
and suddenly you are doing the impossible."
– St. Francis of Assisi

On November 15, 2012, at around 2:37 a.m., came to the world a handsome boy, weighing 4.0 pounds. He was born prematurely via C-section, as he was transversely positioned in his mom's tummy in her eighth month of pregnancy. Had the doctors waited a little bit longer, either the mom or the baby wouldn't have been able to make it due to profuse bleeding. It was an unexpected event, as everything was normal, from conception until before that day when he was born.

Christiann Mikhail is his name, derived from his parents, Christopher and Anna. In honor of the hospital, where he was born and also where Anna was employed at that time, St. Michael's Hospital, there came Mikhail as his second name.

I can still vividly remember that very early hour of the day while lying on the operating table, illuminated by the surgical light and still feeling groggy and tired, when the nicest music came to my ear—my Christiann's cries. A stream of tears poured down from my very swollen eyes—a bucket, I could recall. I was just so happy; we were both alive! Praise God!

Happy days had passed until something peculiar happened upon waking up one morning. I felt anxious and confused about myself. Thinking that it was related to sleepless nights from frequent awakenings and breastfeeding, I sought help from my household. Albeit I had their assistance, nothing changed in my mood; I was still feeling down and depressed, really depressed. But now you ask, "Why feel depressed when you and Christiann were alive and well?" Yeah, right.

I was diagnosed with Postpartum Depression (PPD), also known as Postnatal Depression, which is a mood disorder associated with childbirth. I had consistent crying episodes triggered by unknown reasons, as well as extreme sadness, low energy, and irritability. A serious condition, yet oftentimes taken for granted.

I'm a fighter, I know. And I told myself, "This cannot continue for long. I have four kids now and a husband to take care of—plus myself, of course. I'm going to lose the battle if I don't choose to break the chain."

I browsed the internet—Googled as we say—risk factors related to PPD, and how to treat it. From the list I found, one struck me that said, "Write it down." I suddenly felt enthused because I love to write.

I had finally figured out where this depression was coming from. And that was the fact that I wanted to be a full-time, stay-at-home mom (SAHM).

But I asked, "How? When?" I didn't know where to start.

Others say that the strongest emotional trigger that can move a person is pain, which I could consciously relate to. I was in a strong amount of pain, which became my biggest "WHY."

Then came November of 2013, and I went back to my full-time job in the hospital. There were still bouts of mood swings but not as bad as before. However, there was still some pain going on inside of me. Leaving my Christiann at home because of my corporate job was really, really painful. So, I made a decision to quit my job that I really loved, but it was not abrupt. With my husband's support, we planned and put a timeline of four years, just before Christiann goes to junior kindergarten, in September of 2016.

In May of 2016, we went to Israel to celebrate my 40th birthday, with a side trip to Florence and Assisi, Italy. It was a dream come true for me, where I perfectly felt to have had a close encounter with God. I pleaded in prayer for about 11 days during the Holy Mass in Assisi, St. Francis's hometown. "Lord, give me a sign," I prayed. No sign, nothing whatsoever. However, on the 12th day, in his sermon, the priest said, "Love God through your family." Spot on! I hear you, Lord. It was confirmed, and an answered prayer for me.

With proper planning and some trade-offs, I was able to leave my corporate job, though with a heavy heart, on August 16, 2016. That was the day I officially declared myself as a stay-at-home mom, because I really am! It felt good. Just in time before Santino's, my third child, and Christiann's school opens in September.

Let me share with you what I've done and how I did it. I'd also like to guide you on how to create multiple income streams, while being present with your family at home.

I am a mommy, and I really mean business.

So, please keep reading, as my journey starts here...

Chapter 1
Working from Home Myths Debunked

Making Money From Home Can't Be a Real Business

I'd been initially sold by the notion that a business can only be considered as such when it's being operated in a brick-and-mortar establishment, where customers physically come and transact.

It used to be the literal definition of a business during the Industrial Age, until the Digital or Information Age came, whereby anything can be done virtually through the internet at any given time and anywhere you are.

A traditional business normally operates during typical *business hours* only, while an online business can run 24/7, with no limitations with regard to its location because everything is done online from start to finish.

During the early outset of online businesses, in the early 2000s, it was part of the argument that small business owners cannot compete with big corporations. However, the trend changed and continues to change every day due to the introduction of social media platforms that are extremely famous online and are now readily available in just a few clicks. And the best part is that they are free to use.

In the realm of a traditional business, services are only limited in that specific geographic location for its target market unless it is a very specialized business that caters a unique service or product, where customers go to you to get it; that then makes them regular patrons. However, in today's business operations, such that you can compete in the online arena, a business owner or a service provider has to go where people go. And social media platforms serve that purpose very well.

Let's take, for instance, the very famous Facebook. Millions upon millions are its active users. It has now become the most widely used medium by every business owner, big or small, to bring their products and services right in front of their customers, 24/7. Due to the continuous evolvement of technological advancement, it is important to provide the solution to the customers' problems, or exactly what they are looking for.

I know a lot of very successful online entrepreneurs who make a lot of money from selling both physical and digital products on the internet, from anywhere they are in the world.

Needless to say, making money from home is a real business, even if it's not operated in the traditional way (brick-and-mortar) because it's usually done online.

In my case, I have my own home office space, exclusively designated for my work and business, legitimate business name registration, updated and proper tax filing every year, financial statement, office equipment and supplies, etc.

Yes, I work from home, but I operate a business—a real business.

In that sense, a business, regardless of its size, can be successfully operated wherever you are as long as there's a transaction going on between you as the business owner and the customer.

Online Business Is a Scam

I'm part of the general population who was initially scared of doing anything online. Just because the internet can provide almost everything you need to know, a lot of people are becoming more cautious about suspicious, fraudulent activities online. I couldn't blame them, simply because it's really prevalent. And that's where due diligence plays a very, very important role. There are so many get-rich-quick schemes that victims fall prey to online scammers, which tend to create many misguided notions about an online business, and subsequently affects the genuine ones.

And because not everybody is keen in determining which one is fraudulent or not, I will share some tips that will help you spot scams:

- Promising huge profits without any effort needed.
- When it sounds too good to be true.
- Unsecure websites (e.g., absence of "https" in the address bar).
- A lot of pop-up ads on the website.
- Unable to locate information of the business (e.g., physical address, contact information, etc.).

- Using flashy car images with huge mansions, piles of money, etc.
- Shady online reviews.
- No clear business registration by any regulating body.
- Asking for your personal and credit card information upfront.
- Asking for money through an untraceable route.

Now, I will share with you the best practices to prevent yourself from being victimized by online scammers:

- Don't be quickly lured by suspicious promises of generating huge income without having to take action on your part.
- When it sounds too good to be true, it probably is. Practice due diligence and investigate further.
- On the website, look for the "s" (a secure socket layer) after the "http," which means that the communication between your browser and the website you're visiting is encrypted and/or protected.
- Not only that too many pop-up ads are annoying and disruptive when visiting a website, it is also a big red flag. Legitimate businesses know that ads can drive away prospective customers and may look unprofessional. Never click on any pop-up ads.
- Always look for the *Contact Us* tab when visiting a website, especially for a business. If calling the number listed is possible, it will help you a lot in your investigation. Locating their physical address, as well as online, would be a very good way to spot if it's a scam or not.

- People want proof, which is not bad. However, most of the online scammers use fake images that are easy to copy from somewhere else.
- While reviews online can be fabricated, it is also one of the best ways to know if a business is good or bad, or even a scam. Always check for major review sites and see what people are saying about it.
- A legitimate business should always be registered by its regulating body. If no registration can back it up, it deserves further investigation by a more in-depth research.
- I'm personally scared to provide my pertinent personal identifier to anybody whom I don't personally know, especially online. The same is true when credit card or bank information is asked for. It's better to be extra careful than sorry.
- Sometimes scammers go as far as asking to transfer money through fraudulent recipients to hide their true identity. A specific example is an email transfer, wire transfer, or remittance through a financial institution.
- Never let your hard-earned money slip out of your hands that easy.

To wrap it all up, I have to say that anything can possibly happen online. Operations happening on the internet can't be controlled, and sometimes it's hard to determine which is a scam or not. But I also have to say that not all businesses operated online are a scam.

I do my businesses online, and I'm very confident that what I do is not a scam.

Income From Home Is Unsustainable

There's this notion that income can only be considered legitimate when it's derived from a regular 9-to-5 job.

Here's the thing.

The difference between an active income from typical employment and an income from a business operated at home is whether it is fixed or variable. In other words, when you're employed, and it is fixed income, you have already pre-determined how much salary you'll get according to the position you applied for. On the other hand, in the case of an income from home that varies, it gives a lot of people the impression that it cannot be sustained.

I have to say that this argument now becomes irrelevant, especially because, these days, a lot of online entrepreneurs are becoming self-made millionaires in a shorter period of time. This only proves that income from home can make a person rich faster than regular employees who are only earning a fixed salary.

You may recall I have previously mentioned that we are in the Information Age, where digital products and services are a very hot commodity these days. Online business owners create and sell these types of products to solve a particular problem, for which customers are very much willing to pay for, sometimes at a very high cost.

I quit my job, and my businesses that I now run from home are very sustainable, to the point that my revenues from the different streams I created replaced my 9-to-5 job income.

However, I have to make a disclaimer that not every business is the same in terms of revenues and results. Some owners can generate an attractive income much faster, while others don't. But the good news is, when you have an operating business that doesn't really generate an income that you expect, there is always room for improvement. Little tweaks are usually the missing part to realize a more attractive conversion or sales.

Here's my advice:

First, it is significantly important that you try to know what type or nature of business you intend to operate at home. Second, it is highly recommended that you have a coach who is more knowledgeable than yourself, or has successfully done the same type of business that you're interested in. Third, always invest in self-improvement to know more about the latest trend; the reality is that what's working today may already be obsolete tomorrow.

There Is Work-Life Balance

Let me give you a realistic expectation with regard to work-life balance, especially when we talk about working from home.

Running your own business at home is actually tough at the outset, from setting up to establishing a routine that best works for you. Yes, I agree that there's this little flexibility, but work-life balance can't be initially expected, and can only be afforded once a system is successfully put in place.

But before we delve more into discussing further, what does work-life balance mean to you?

I had to admit that I was initially quite perplexed by its meaning.

According to Wikipedia, *"Work-life balance is the term used to describe the balance that an individual needs between time allocated for work and other aspects of life. Areas of life other than work-life can be, but not limited to, personal interests, family and social or leisure activities."*

You know that I had this strong inclination to leave my corporate job, and that I would rather be a stay-at-home mom. Because of this, it's now quite clear to me what work-life balance means. In other words, it's simply doing things that you love, in good proportion. There's always time for work, family, self, and other activities.

And so, I have to say that the meaning of work-life balance can vary from person to person.

In my own experience, just because I'd started off as a one-man show, operating my home business was really difficult. As there was no Bundy clock for time in and time out, I would always tend to work longer than one would normally spend in the 9-to-5 working hours as an employee. I had no reliever in the event that I wanted to take a vacation, or even to have a break for a few minutes. However, the main difference that I really do appreciate is the flexibility, which I've previously mentioned. I'm in perfect control of my time and have the ability to spend it the way I want.

It Kills The Corporate Culture

And you ask, "What does this corporate culture mean?"

According to Investopedia, *"Corporate culture refers to the beliefs and behaviors that determine how a company's employees and management interact and handle outside business transactions. Often, a corporate culture is implied, not expressly defined, and develops organically over time from the cumulative traits of the people that the company hires. A company's culture will be reflected in its dress code, business hours, office setup, employee benefits, turnover, hiring decisions, treatment of clients, client satisfaction, and every other aspect of operations."*

In my own words, this simply means that every business entity has its own unique way of operating on a daily basis, whereby it involves a team's collaboration with either flexible or assigned roles of each member to reach to the very core of a company's ideology, practice, mission and vision, and practices.

And now the question is, "Does corporate culture happen in a work-from-home setting?"

First, when you come to think about home-based work, what comes to mind is a one-man show, versus a group of people working together as a team. Although this may literally be true, working in a home setting doesn't always mean that there are no other individuals involved to operate its business.

I am one specific example of this. I do work physically from home by myself, but I also have a team that I hired to virtually do certain tasks for a more productive and efficient result.

Although I may not need to wear corporate attire when running my own business, it doesn't mean that the corporate spirit is absent. Since I am the main authority for my business regulations and policies, I see to it that everyone in my virtual team follows the business culture that I set before them. I also make sure that everyone knows the specific acceptable behaviors related to the outcome of our services that we offer to our clients and, of course, to the integrity of our company name.

You see, there's really no difference with regard to exercising a corporate culture, whether you are in a traditional corporate office or in a home setting. Although others treat working remotely as a career suicide, I very strongly disagree with that. I've attended self-development workshops and courses online, which I also encourage my virtual team to do.

Do you know that several corporations are now shifting to this type of work setting, whereby their employees can work from home, such as IBM, Cisco, etc.?

In essence, I believe that every career-driven individual has the same opportunity regardless of the location in which the business entity operates. Thanks to our advanced technology!

It's a One-Size-Fits-All Deal

Everyone is different in terms of preference, situation, needs, etc. I am a mom, and you may also be a mom. But we may perform tasks in our respective households in different ways and styles.

Do we have a manual to follow? Of course, we don't! How I cook my pasta may be different from the way you do yours, but the result is still the same.

The same is true with choosing between being a career woman in a corporate office setting and a business owner who is operating from home. But please, let me clarify this first. There's no wrong choice here.

Why do I say this?

I can clearly say that working from home is not for everyone. What works for me may not work for you. However, the good news is that your initial choice is not permanent. It can be changed overtime as you see fit.

.

Chapter 2
Life's Rhythm

Different Attacks

In both work-from-home and corporate settings, workers experience life's rhythm that is sometimes displayed in a particular pattern triggered by some stimuli, such as an event, environment, person, or just by any unknown reason under the sun.

Let me share with you some very common bouts of combined physical, emotional, physiological, etc., attacks in any given work environment.

- Panic attacks.
- Anxiety attacks.
- Vulnerability attacks.
- Laziness attacks.
- Burnout attacks.

You may notice that the words, before the word, *attacks*, are pretty much negative.

When panic and anxiety attacks strike, there's a sudden feeling of terror, without a warning. A specific trigger for these kinds of attacks, related to work, can be a pile of paperwork that needs to meet a certain deadline. It can also be brought about by an unhappy customer, with your fear of either getting fired or losing a business transaction. Manifestations vary physiologically, such as breathing difficulties, numbness of some body parts, chest pains, cold sweats, racing heart, and a lot more.

Vulnerability attacks normally happen when you feel like you are struggling in an area or two. This type of attack can also happen in both work settings. When I'm alone performing my day-to-day business tasks, and I can't seem to get anybody in my time zone to work for me, or with me, because most of my team members are on the other side of the globe, I tend to feel less productive and inefficient—thus vulnerable. The same holds true for the corporate world. Instead of trying to do it all, you can certainly ask for help from your colleagues to come up with your desired result.

This now becomes too obvious for me when laziness attacks strike, as I work close to my bedroom. Or when I don't feel like going to my computer, and I watch TV instead. So, how do I get myself past that stage? Although it's easier said than done, I try to exercise discipline, and implement proper time management. Are you convinced? Yes, I think sometimes it's not bad to follow that kind of indulgence to just lie down and be a couch-potato for some time. But honest to God, I do really have that attack, and I'll not deny that. And I've not known anybody in my lifetime to have been spared from laziness at some point in their working life, either in an office setting or at home.

When you do something that you love, feeling burned out seldom occurs, or not at all. This only becomes evident when an employee hates his job, his boss, his colleagues, or even himself. He just hates everything in his environment.

It's not my case. I quit my job albeit I loved it. I decided to transition because I thought it was the better choice for me and my family.

Routines and Rituals

There are a couple of patterns that I think can help us structure our lives appropriately, through routines and rituals. Oftentimes they are mistaken as the same, but in reality they are different.

Routines can be best described by what we do on a daily basis immediately after we rise up from bed. My best example for this is my beauty and self-care routines that I do every day.

Rituals, on the other hand, are simply known as traditional activities that are not done on quite a regular basis like that of routines. These are rather best described as ceremonial types of activities that can bring transformation in perceptions, experiences, or perspectives. My best example for this is going to the Holy Mass once a week for my spiritual nourishment. It can also be best described by going to yoga classes once in a while for health purposes.

I have a list of my routines and rituals. What about you?

In essence, we need routines and rituals that work best for our needs, so that we can enjoy life as it is.

How to Not Lose Your Mind

At some point, I'm feeling overwhelmed. Honestly. I bet we all surely do! Family and work, work and family, plus the extra thousands of things happening on the side. Keeping ourselves calm is the best way to stay sane.

But how do I do that? Here's my list:

- Find enough sleep to feel energized and prepared for the next day.
- Plan out your day ahead of time.
- Have at least 5 minutes of exercise before starting your day.
- Eat right and on time. Drink lots of water.
- Take breaks in between tasks.
- Ask for help when feeling overwhelmed. Don't do all things alone.
- Socialize as much as you can.
- Do journaling every day.

Being a mom is a tough, 24/7 job, without any time off. You're always on call. Although I know everyone in my household is dependent on me, I still have to make sure that I take care of myself as well, because if I become incapable of providing all the best I can to my loved ones, it becomes more problematic. Because of that, I should find exclusive time for myself, which brings me down to the next item: My Me Time.

My Me Time

When I got married to my wonderful husband, and we had children of our own, they became my first priorities. It's a non-negotiable deal to me. However, I have a set of activities that I do for myself as soon as I'm able.

When the kids are already at school and my husband goes off to work, I'm left with no one for the day but me, myself, and I. And here are the things that I do during *My Me Time*.

- Worship and prayer time (Bible reading and worship songs)
- Self-development time (reading books, online workshops, etc.)
- Entertainment time (social media, YouTube, TV, etc.)
- Indulgence time (coffee and snacks)
- Rest time (power nap, etc.)
- Short walks, weather-permitting

Although these different times are basically done routinely, they're actually spread out throughout the day. These are my little ways to still find time for myself, which help me boost my productivity and re-charge my wellbeing. These can also sometimes feed my child-like yearnings, which I really find helpful and healthy.

Because I know I've been unloading a lot to effectively serve my family on a daily basis, I realized that I also need to feed my personal needs so that I can continue to serve them enthusiastically and energetically.

I'm Still a Human Being

Experiencing life's rhythm on a daily basis is real proof that we are indeed humans, which separates us from other living creatures. Although a mom is known for being an expert in multi-tasking, she is still a human being, not a machine. But even then, a machine still gets tired. When a computer crashes, it just raises a signal that it can only take as much work as it can. Why? There's this so-called threshold by which one can operate only to a certain point of acceptable functionality.

The same holds true for human beings like you and me.

The Four Seasons of Motherhood

There is a particular set or sequence of seasons, not only applicable to a given calendar year but also in a person's life, specifically for mothers, which I call *The Four Seasons of Motherhood.*

My existence used to be so plain and simple before my married life, as there was no mountain of responsibility on my plate yet. Although every mom's journey is different, I can only be sure of one thing: there are seasons in every mother's life.

In the same way when the earth moves around the sun, we know that a particular season of the year is coming. When winter is over, spring should come next; then comes fall, and then summer follows.

Motherhood works the same way. Please let me describe the Four Seasons of Motherhood, which I have described according to my own experience:

- Infancy Stage Season.
- Toddler Stage Season.
- Teenager Stage Season.
- Adulthood Stage Season.

You become a mother the moment you know you're pregnant with your first child, and that's my infancy stage season. It's the early stage where a mom-to-be gets to embrace that great sense of motherhood as though the child were already born, which requires physical, mental, and emotional preparedness.

Once the child is born, here comes the toddler stage season. A mom's life's rhythm abruptly changes because this is now where the actual action starts. Imagine a toddler who just starts to walk. A brand-new mom also develops her skills as days go by and, for the most part, becomes creative. The toddler stage season in motherhood are the tough days, which are hard enough that they physically drain you due to a lot of action going on. This is where a typical mom becomes panicky due to certain fears of her child getting hurt from falling, slipping on the floor, etc.

The teenager stage season brings more of a mixed emotion, for me as a mom, when we talk about the physical and emotional side of things. Since they are now quite independent physically, and can do most things on their own, I don't really need to be hands-on with them. However, emotionally speaking, I find it quite challenging to understand their mood swings and tantrums.

Adulthood stage season is when all our kids leave the house and live somewhere else, away from home due to studies or to settle down. Because I'm not there yet, I'll not put too much emphasis on this.

You may ask, "What do these seasons have to do with working from home?"

My answer is, "A whole lot." Why? You may recall that I found it hard to decipher between leaving my corporate job and working from home. Had I been in the infancy stage season, I'm pretty sure that transition would be extremely hard due to factors such as resources, time constraints, etc. Also, you can imagine how your work conditions would look when you have a toddler, who needs your full attention, running around the house. However, it still depends on your situation, which I have also previously mentioned. You may still opt to not leave your corporate job while being at this stage, as long as you can find assistance with childcare, etc.

I intently described these four seasons of motherhood so that it could help you arrive at your desired decision with regard to work and/or business; and, of course, according to your specific situation.

Chapter 3
Queen of My Bees-Nest (or Busy-Nest): Homemaking

"Think like a queen. A queen is not afraid to fail. Failure is another steppingstone to greatness."
– Oprah Winfrey

My Daily Grind

Homemaking is a tough job but a rewarding one. I'm the queen bee of my beehive. I'm always busy doing stuff for my nest.

I'm not just a stay-at-home mom but also a working mom at home. Either way, I have to do things daily to love and serve my family first. Prioritizing them over myself is already part of the deal.

When I was in the infancy stage season of my motherhood, and learning stuff firsthand, everything changed: priorities, mindset, habits, preferences, needs, and the list goes on. I, myself, even changed—I believe, for the better—as a person, a wife, and a mom.

How does my daily grind look, in a household of six (four kids plus myself and my husband)?

Apart from doing the household chores, my very most important goal is to be always present to the five of them, all the time, if at all possible. My daily grind starts with showing love the moment I wake up, through the food I feed them, the dishes I clean as they leave, and the clothes I launder, etc.

My goal, as the queen of our nest, is to maintain our house as a haven of peace, love, and harmony.

A Wife First, A Mom Second

I have always believed that as successful followers of Christ, establishing the correct priorities in our lives is highly important. The scriptural order of priorities, being God as the first one, should look like this: spouse, children, parents, extended family, brothers and sisters in Christ, and then the rest of the world.

I cannot stress highly enough what marriage can do to two people. It changes everything when it comes to the dynamics of a family. A mom's homemaking responsibility immediately starts on the day she gets married, which makes her the official wife to her husband, as she prepares for a more exciting stage of her family life. Because the strong anchor is held between that tie that connects a man and a woman together, a wife has the ability to strengthen that bond by making her husband the priority in her life.

Thus, I'm a wife first.

When I'd talk to others and the topic would be about priorities, eyebrows would start to raise after saying the last line. I feel them, and I cannot even blame them either. I also used to believe otherwise.

But you know what? When a couple clearly understands each role at the beginning of their marriage, and where they stand in each other's lives, the question with regard to priorities shouldn't be a real problem or an issue, because the reality is that couples are supposed to be extensions of themselves to serve one another and their children.

Although I'm the queen of my household, decisions are still made together with collaborated actions.

I'm also a mom. And it's a fact.

Keeping the Place

Our home isn't just a dwelling place; it's a haven. Everything that happens inside our haven is sacred as we collect our precious memories as a family. And as the queen bee of my nest, I also have that sacred role to keep it in order, not just physically but in all aspects.

So, how do I do that? Here's my short list of the basics:

- Making sure that the basic needs are well supplied
- Financial obligations are well taken care of
- Important appointments are attended to
- Maintaining a nice breathing environment inside and outside the house
- De-cluttering as needed

- Maintaining peace, love, and harmony around the house
- Discussing conflicts within family members
- Keeping family affairs private
- Going out as a family
- Helping each other out regardless of the circumstance
- Respecting each other's individuality, uniqueness, and privacy

I Don't Have My Master's Degree

Being a homemaker doesn't require any certification, much less a master's degree. It doesn't even exclude any woman from being qualified to perform the job as a homemaker. Homemaking is not only the toughest job on earth but also the most rewarding. And that one job needs mastery of skills to perfectly run a household, not a degree.

So, fellow moms, if at some point you feel like you're not good enough for the job, don't fret. You may also sometimes feel inadequate, and less like mommy material, or worse, a bad mom.

Remember that we're not born as mothers; we become mothers.

It's Dark When the Light Is Off

My biological mother is the domesticated type of a woman. She is, in fact, my role model and one of my greatest influencers. I witnessed how she ran our household and how she managed to keep everything organized. She knows everything—literally everything—when you ask her where to find this and that, how to do things from scratch, and so forth. As a result, we were totally dependent on her, until she had a motor vehicle accident, years ago, that left us all paralyzed.

Moms are considered to be the life and the light of every home. In a real sense, absence of a glow in a dark spot can be really gloomy. Imagine not having a mom in every household. I can surely bet that it would be really chaotic, unorganized, and messy.

I'm a wife to my very supportive husband, and a mom to our four wonderful kids. And I can imagine how difficult it would be for them if I were always away due to my 9-to-5 job. My sad experience with my mom being absent for some time, due to an accident, influenced me to think about staying at home so that I could completely fulfill my duties and responsibilities to my own family, as a wife and as a mom. .

I finally did it. And here's my best reward.

My Best Reward

Nothing in this world can compensate a woman's ability to take care of her family full-time while doing business in the comfort of her own home. And this is my best reward. I'm flexible. I'm free. I'm happy. It's my ultimate dream as a wife and as a mom, let alone as an entrepreneur. I'm enjoying both worlds!

I've had some trade-offs to realize my dream, and it wasn't easy. But it's all worth it.

Chapter 4
Let's Get You Started

Do you know that YOU are your biggest problem? But do YOU also know that you are your biggest asset? Contradictory but true. It's how you see yourself, which can either make or break you.

Most of our problems are self-inflicted. Why did I say that? It's just a matter of perspective and how one responds to a certain situation.

Let me tell you a story.

Scenario 1:

A man was driving to work when suddenly he was struck from behind by another vehicle. Fortunately, he was not harmed. His anger caused him to curse the other driver. He went back to his car, and continued driving on his way to work. He continued to be angry, even at his workplace, causing him to complain about everything with everyone he would come across. His 9-to-5 shift at work that day ended, and he went home but was still feeling unwell and angry. His wife and kids attempted to kiss him when he came through the door, but he wasn't in a good enough mood to even say "Hi" to his family. He ended up going straight to the bedroom, not eating his dinner, and falling asleep until it was time to wake up for another shift at work the next day.

Scenario 2:

A man was driving to work when suddenly he was struck from behind by another vehicle. Fortunately, he was not harmed. He was so thankful about the fact that despite the near-death experience, he was alive and well. He went back to his car and continued driving to work. Because of his gratefulness, he greeted everyone when he arrived at his workplace, smiled at his colleagues, and just felt grateful about everything. His 9-to-5 shift at work ended, and he went home, maintaining his happy mood. His wife and kids attempted to kiss him when he came through the door, and he jumped for joy seeing them altogether, as they said, "Hi." He ended up telling his family about what had happened and that he was saved. They ate dinner together, and he went to sleep to be ready for his shift at work the next day.

You see, these two men had the same scenarios. Could you tell the huge difference between them?

Yes, it was the way they responded to the same incident.

Don't get me wrong. Anger is not bad, and expressing it doesn't make you a bad person either. But let me tell you that what makes it bad is how you respond or deal with it and what you do about it. So the question is, "Will you stay being angry, or will you do something about that anger to make things better?"

In this chapter, we will only be focusing on the six (6) facets of your wellbeing: Mental, Emotional, Physical, Social, Spiritual, and Financial Wellbeing. These make up your personality.

Let's get started.

Mental Wellbeing

From the medical perspective, the central nervous system (CNS) controls most functions of the body and mind, which consists of two main parts: the spinal cord and the brain. Since we will be talking about one's mental wellbeing, we'll only focus on the one part that controls it, which is the BRAIN. The brain is the center of our thoughts, the interpreter of our external environment, and the origin of control over body movements.

From this alone, we know how crucial it is to seriously take care of our thoughts, such as those things we should embrace or entertain, and what we should get rid of or ignore. Going back to my story that I mentioned above, scenarios 1 and 2, the outcomes were very different. One simple thought that dictates the kind of response to the event may either ruin the whole day or divert to something better, which makes a very huge difference that can make or break you.

We also use our mental wellbeing to form our mindset. In other words, we can establish a set of attitudes or a way of thinking and opinions based on what we've learned from personal experience or from others through coaching and mentorship. It is the very reason why it is also crucial who we listen to and hang out with because our environment can greatly affect our own mindset.

Create a culture of greatness in you through the way you think.

When talking about mindset, I can also include goals (be it personal, career, spiritual, or financial). With my set goals and timeline to target, I've come up with structuring a roadmap to achieve them.

My goal: to be a stay-at-home mom and create several income streams at home.

My timeline: in four years' time after giving birth to Christiann.

My recommendations to maintain a healthy mental wellbeing include:

- Love and value yourself first.
- Look at things positively in every circumstance.
- Don't overload your mind.
- Do mindfulness and meditation therapies.
- Get enough sleep.
- Surround yourself with positive people.
- Write it down.
- Talk to someone you trust.
- Forgive yourself and others.
- Laugh and celebrate.
- Be grateful all the time.

Emotional Wellbeing

Another significant trait, of which humans are considered to be superior over animals, is the belief that animals do not have emotions. I'm not quite sure about this, and it is not really scientifically proven, but I think we express our emotions better than animals.

There is, in fact, a debate among professionals such as scientists, through their study, that we should not assume animals do think and have emotions. However, there is another study, which is featured on the National Geographic channel, online, that animals indeed think and have emotions.

Although there hasn't been a specific answer to this, what I know is that every creature has emotions—even plants do! But I cannot be certain how they react to a given stimulus because we don't know their world. They must have their own way of thinking, feeling, communicating, etc. I just don't know.

But this is what I, myself, believe: that every living thing can feel, and that a feeling is directly connected to emotions.

For us humans, Intelligence Quotient, or what we all know as IQ, is used as a parameter to test a person's reasoning ability or cognitive capacity relative to his or her peers. Albert Einstein (a German-born theoretical physicist), among others, was known to have a very high IQ score. However, because people are more likely to be interested in one's intelligence, they most of the time fail to recognize that there is this one very important human ability, called Emotional Quotient, or EQ.

You may recall that the brain dictates the human behaviors. It is also important to note that emotions work together with our mindset.

What is Emotional Quotient, or EQ?

It is the level of a person's emotional intelligence, and the capability of an individual to recognize his or her emotions and those of others, discern between different feelings and label them appropriately, use emotional information to guide thinking and behavior, and manage and/or adjust emotions to adapt to environments or achieve one's goal (s).

We often hear this line: Don't make a decision when you're extremely emotional.

Why? Because you can screw up. Decision-making is usually influenced by logic (IQ) and emotions (EQ).

My recommendations to maintain your healthy emotional wellbeing would be:

- Delay in making a major decision when extremely emotional.
- Keep silent when emotionally distraught, as it can hurt yourself or others.
- Again, write it down.
- Socialize and talk to someone you trust.
- Get over it.
- Take a walk.
- Think before you act.
- Stay calm and relax.

Physical Wellbeing

"Do you not know that your bodies are temples of the Holy Spirit, who is in you, whom you have received from God? You are not your own." (1 Cor. 6:19)

After we have taken care of what's inside, let's now go to the outside: our physical body.

If we reflect on the passage above, from the Holy Bible, we are told to take care of our physical body because that's where the Holy Spirit dwells. The fact that we don't own it, we are liable for any damages incurred due to misuse and abuse. In other words, it's our responsibility to take care of our body because it's not ours in the first place. Living a healthy lifestyle, practicing good hygiene, etc., are some of the common practices for self-care and good physical wellness.

So, how do we really take care of our bodies?

- Eat healthy food.
- Drink lots of water.
- Exercise regularly.
- Dump sugars.

Remember, you are what you eat.

Social Wellbeing

I may be wrong, but I assume that you're likely reading this book because you're considering to work and do business from home. And it literally means that you'll be saved from the usual office politics in the corporate world. However, online entrepreneurs, like me, feel the need to interact with people socially, either online or offline.

As humans are known to be naturally social, we need others to tell and share our stories with, or even our frustrations about anything. However, we should be very mindful about whom we connect with, as it can be detrimental to our growth, both in terms of personal and business.

We can maintain our healthy social wellbeing by the following:

- Seeking support from our primary sources.
- Staying socially connected to positive people.
- Reaching out to mentors for self-growth.

Our primary source obviously can be our spouse or significant other, or even a relative or a friend.

Don't isolate yourself from the world. Stay connected to grow socially.

Spiritual Wellbeing

Because our world today has too much noise and chaos, we tend to neglect this one very important aspect of humans: spiritual health and wellness that can greatly affect one's overall wellbeing.

Maintaining a sound spiritual wellbeing directs us to a beautiful way of living that can then result to better health outcomes and expectations. Spirituality doesn't merely talk about pure religion or just any spiritual practices and beliefs, but rather it can involve a better understanding, and finding a person's own sense of deeper meaning and purpose in life.

I believe that if a person is well-guided and nurtured spiritually, regardless of religion, he or she can become a seeker of wisdom that helps nurture the stronger foundation in his or her spirit.

So, what enhances a person's spiritual wellbeing? Here's my list:

- Prayer and reflection
- Mindfulness and meditation
- Connecting to nature

Financial Wellbeing

Last but not least, let's talk about our financial wellbeing. I intentionally listed this one as the last item because I believe that a person's current financial standing can directly affect, for the most part, the other aforementioned facets.

I was afraid to quit my job in the first place because it would mean a huge cutback in our household income. It would have been much easier to transition right away from corporate to telecommute if I knew we were already financially secure at that point. My brain was telling me to stay in my job, but my heart was telling me otherwise.

You see, my mental (IQ/logic) and emotional (EQ) facets were fighting against each other because a huge part of my battle involved the financial side of things, which later affected my physical wellbeing. Due to my anxiety attacks and depressive episodes at that time, I was brought to the hospital several times. I had to undergo an MRI to rule out the cause of on-and-off severe headaches.

Had I been left with choices at that time, having to wait for the right time to quit my job that I really loved was immaterial. They say, "Money can't buy happiness." I'd agree somewhat. But what about this? "Money doesn't buy happiness; neither does poverty."

I suggest the following strategies to help maintain a healthy financial wellbeing:

- Assess your financial standing as frequently as possible
- Avoid bad debts, and pay them immediately
- Earn more through multiple income streams
- Save and invest more money
- Build a sound financial house
- Protect yourselves through proper life insurance coverage
- Get a last will and testament done
- Financially prepare before your major shift
- Upgrade your skills for a raise in pay
- Start your own business

Chapter 5
Let's Get You Productive

Targeting Your Timeline

Let's be honest. If I ask you now, "When do you want to quit your job?" OR "When do you want to retire?"

I bet you'll respond, without a doubt, "Right now." But hey, let's be realistic for a second.

I'll be damn straightforward with you. It would be so irresponsible of us if we decided on a very important thing and didn't keep in mind the great implication it could bring to ourselves and our loved ones.

You know, I've had my planning stage, while I was on my maternity leave with my Christiann, in that by the date so and so, I would be out of the corporate world. It took me almost four years, from December of 2012 to August of 2016, and I had to continue listing, writing down, and editing my roadmap when necessary, because of many, many unavoidable circumstances. However, I was still able to make it happen, and target my timeline, despite other factors that had contributed to the changes in the details of the plan.

So, how do you set and target your own timeline?

Well, as I have mentioned, we have to first be realistic and mindful of our very own unique situation. If quitting your job right away will be detrimental to your financial standing, then it is a no-brainer to do it now, unless there are other resources to augment the missing income. From my very own experience, leaving my corporate job caused a huge impact on our finances, which means that the previously two-household income was now only producing one active stream, from my husband's full-time job.

How did I proceed?

Remember I told you that I did not resign from work right away. I had about four years of planning. And in those four years, my husband and I worked harder to create other income streams; we saved and invested, and we did some side hustles to prepare for my most-awaited day, to officially be a stay-at-home mom, on August 16, 2016.

Four years for me would be just the right timeline to say, "Goodbye, boss; hello, freedom!"

It is just fair for me to tell you now that your timeline is dependent on you. But the good news is, you can dictate your own timeline, change it over time, and implement the soonest.

The most important things to remember to do are:

- Be realistic.
- Know where you're currently at.
- Plan out properly.

- Collaborate with your spouse or significant other, including immediate family members.
- Earn more income from different sources.
- Stay focused and determined.
- Stay away from distractions.
- Invest in yourself by engaging in self-development programs.

Managing Your Resources

When you want to start your business, or work from home, you are literally doing it on your own at first. It is a one-man show—just like what I did initially.

You may choose to hire virtual assistants (VAs) to help you, or you may outsource tasks to lessen your workload, which is very reasonably priced and can be very efficient.

However, I used to be the type of person who would try to learn as much as I could, not only to save money but to acquire new knowledge, believing that it's productive and profitable. That may work sometimes, but other aspects of the business may be greatly affected.

In the process, I've realized something. There is a resource, like money, that can be earned back. However, there is another one, a very important one, which is totally gone no matter how hard you try to retrieve it: time.

Your resources: money and time.

Let's briefly talk about *money* first. You may want to go back to the financial wellbeing part, where I discussed about assessing your financial standing, etc.

When I started my writing gigs (blogging, content writing, etc.), I used my old laptop and chose not to buy a new one until my circumstances changed.

I had a friend who bought an expensive laptop for her proposed online business. I can't judge her for that, and I can't even say it's bad. Go ahead when you can afford it. What I'm trying to point out is that it would be much more reasonable if you could wait until you have the results (oftentimes monetary), or maybe buy something not as expensive but can work the same way.

Again, assess where you financially stand, identify your priorities, and go from there.

Let's go ahead and talk about this more important resource, which I believe is *time.*

Have you been asked this question before: "Time or money?"

Can I ask you to pause for a moment and internalize? Given these two options, which is more important for you?

Time or money? Money or time?

Think about this for a second: You have money but no time. Conversely, you have time but no money.

We can be different in our reasoning, but this is my take. I regard time as more important than money, for the following reasons:

- Everyone has only 24 hours in a day, and nobody has the power to add more to it.
- You cannot, at any cost, turn back time.
- Time has no price tag; it's priceless.
- You need time to spend your money.
- When a person is dying, he wishes for more time instead of money.

When working from home, it is important that you manage your time properly for business/work and family.

And the real challenge comes into the picture when, for instance, you're in the middle of completing your business-related tasks and, suddenly, your child comes to you for something, thus interrupting your workflow.

In every endeavor, proper handling of your time, and managing it well, can produce more favorable results.

Here's my very effective suggestion, which I use religiously:

- Plan out ahead of time by creating your personal To-Do list the night before.
- Stop doing things that waste your time.
- Organize tasks according to priorities and deadlines.
- Don't hold for tomorrow what can be done today.
- Don't engage in small talks (e.g., gossip, etc.).
- Spend time with your loved ones as much as possible.

Home-Work Environment

Creating a home-based business doesn't necessarily mean that you get to perform your work tasks exclusively at home.

What does that mean?

Work settings can vary, from a home office, a coffee shop, or a shared working space outside your house, or simply anywhere except in a traditional corporate office setting.

When I was just starting to work from home, I would literally use any part of my house and carry my laptop everywhere. In between household chores, I would normally complete some short tasks because I didn't want to be idle or have my time wasted. Obviously, at the very beginning, I had no designated working space to exclusively do my work or business. However, it worked quite well for some time, but I eventually had to convert our one bedroom to be my formal working space and home office.

And my most favorite perk I have from a home-work environment is that I can still choose to perform tasks, anywhere around the house with my laptop, while defrosting food to get ready for cooking.

Coffee shops also worked well for me, especially when I had a business meeting or had to see a client (s). As you can see, being flexible, not only with my time but with my work settings, is really fun!

I was also once introduced, by another stay-at-home mom entrepreneur who happened to be a close friend of mine, to using a shared working space for a minimal cost. It was a huge office space, with several cubicles, a lounge area, a pantry, and with a complete set of office tools, like a telephone, fax machine, etc. It really looked so corporate and professional that your client wouldn't think it's a shared office space. This setting can give you, as a business owner, that very amazing impression to your clients, which can then convert to more referrals and more income! This may work well for you if a home office space is not possible, or if you feel coffee shops are too public for your business.

I have some tips with regard to the home-work environment for your business:

- A laptop is a must, as it is portable enough to carry anywhere you like.
- Never use your bedroom where you sleep as your working space.
- Put an office table and a chair in one feasible area inside the house.
- De-clutter your working space.
- Learn about basic organizational skills for more productive results.
- Have a backup for storage of important data related to business.
- Register your business appropriately.

Incentives and Rewards

Whether you're an employee or you're your own boss, there are effective ways to enhance productivity with regard to the quality and efficiency of the results.

In our working life, we reach a point where we feel mundane and dull. Being proactive to prevent this from happening in such a way that we don't lose interest in what we do is the way to go.

Other ways include sending your team to upgrade skills by attending leadership and self-development workshops as part of the company's incentives.

Incentives and rewards don't have to be expensive and fancy. I feel more productive when I give myself a break by just going out for a coffee and a donut, or eating at my favorite restaurant to celebrate anything I've accomplished related to my business. It's merely telling your subconscious mind through your physical actions that "hey, you did a great job!"

I also give incentives to my team when a project is finished perfectly well before the deadline. This doesn't only boost their morale but also makes them more inspired to do their jobs even better. Treat yourself and your teammates very well, and they will in turn take care of your business consciously.

The whole idea is to celebrate every milestone, big or small. It invites good vibes and naturally pushes more to perform even better by investing quite a bit for massive and favorable results.

Old School Still Works

Productivity can still increase significantly, even offline, by simply reading a book, exactly like what you're doing now. Congratulations!

I admit that I still have that part of me who's old-fashioned in certain areas. Why old-fashioned? Almost everybody I know uses hand-held devices for just about anything. But I'm not one of them. I'm not a very big fan of electronic devices to track my productivity either.

The perfect combination of a pen and paper works perfectly fine for me. I'm a savings addict. Uh oh, I'm kind of cheap. Recycling old stuff is my favorite way to save. For instance, old notebooks with unused pages; I'd put them together and re-use. Another example is the free store calendars, or the downloadable version from the internet, which I enjoy using to see my schedule for the whole month at a glance!

I'm also a big fan of sticky notes, a small but terrible item that saves me most of the time when I tend to miss out on a date, a bill payment, or an event.

And how can I forget my To-Do list! I'd make sure to make one the night before my next day of actions. It serves as my secretary—no complaints, no salary! My life is easier that way, isn't it?

Other Useful Tools

Sorry, I lied. I just said that I'm the old-fashioned type of person who doesn't really like to use electronic devices to track productivity.

I know for a fact that technology continues to evolve and change every day. Not following what's in, or the latest, will kill your business in no time. I'm not just making up a story; I've seen a lot that ended up landing to this unfortunate ending.

As I continue to explore through further research, mentorships, newsletters, and other materials available online and offline, there are very useful online tools to keep track of your business's progress.

In the case of an affiliate and an online marketer, building an e-mail list is mandatory. It is considered to be your money machine when a product or an offer is ready to be broadcasted. Collecting an e-mail list can be effective by using the so-called Autoresponder. It is a service that allows you to automatically send out e-mails to a group or several groups of people, which can be set in sequence at certain intervals, i.e., every day, once a week, or on an as-needed basis. The collected e-mail addresses are stored in your selected Autoresponder (e.g., Aweber, GetResponse, MailChimp, etc.), for a flat fee monthly, depending on your chosen plan. MailChimp is the only free service provider I know but it can store only a limited number of e-mail addresses.

Another tool that I now use is ManyChat. It is a Facebook Messenger bot (free and paid versions) that can serve as a real-time chat bot. In other words, the other party may think that he/she is talking to you live. ManyChat can broadcast messages, has analytics, schedules postings in sequence, as well as having other features. It can also collect subscribers once your prospects click on the messages or videos you post. In addition, it can be personalized by using its features, whereby you can automatically capture the first name of your subscriber.

You may have also heard about Google Analytics. But I won't be explaining more about it because I didn't use it, and I'm not comfortable in detailing something I'm not familiar with.

There are far more productivity tools available online that you will definitely benefit from, and I'll give you the freedom to check for yourself.

Chapter 6
Let's Get You Known

Branding is Key

Look and observe your surroundings. Everything has a name. Every person is given a name. You have a name, and I have a name. Why? Because a name serves as an important identifier. It becomes automatically attached to you or a certain thing, or even an event.

A name may mean nothing to many. However, if you're a company, a business owner, a service provider, a speaker, an author, a product endorser, or a celebrity, and you want to be known for what you promise to your customers or audience, you need to do something very, very important: branding.

Branding is your specific identity that when it's mentioned, it automatically associates with you or your company. A brand name is so important that it depicts a promise to your customers, and it usually represents what your products or services stand for.

You may say that your business is too small for branding, or you're not good enough to be branded. You have to remember that we do business to earn, and earning just enough isn't a good goal. Brand strategy gives you a major edge in competitive markets these days. Your brand is basically derived from who you are and what your values are.

Here are my specific examples of brand names, where their promises stick and stand out:

- Walmart: "Save money. Live better."
- Disney: "Creating happiness through magical experiences."
- Honda: "The power of dreams."
- Spotify: "Music for everyone."
- Levi's: "Quality never goes out of style."

And for my transcription business:

- Trans-ACTS & Communications: "Quality and Efficient Transcription Delivered."

Essentially, it's really dangerous for a brand to not live up to its promises. To overdeliver means to create "WOW" moments for your customers. And that's one of the most effective ways to build your army of loyal customers, who will then create another layer of loyal and happy customers through word of mouth and direct referrals, which means more conversion to sales; thus, more income!

Be on Top of Your Game

Being in the know, or at least getting yourself updated all the time, gives you a huge edge among the rest in your competition. Knowing what's trending saves you from being left behind. Innovation is also important. Be different. Be unique.

If you're in sales and are offering products and services, create your Unique Selling Proposition (USP) that stands out. Let your customers be your walking ads.

Knowledge is power, and more so when it's applied. Reading books related to your niche, self-development, leadership materials, and the like, can bring wisdom. The information you acquire by educating yourself can be used to your tactical advantage just before it becomes a common knowledge to the average person in your chosen field. Continuously studying your niche is a priceless investment. Be ahead of the game by incessant learning.

However, reading is not enough. You have to implement what you've read! And this is why a lot get stuck.

The Power of Social Media

Marketing your business or yourself as the brand can produce lucrative results when you're exposed to your target market. As a business owner or a service provider, it is mandatory that you get to be known.

Most entrepreneurs, big and small, use social media to market themselves or their business. It has changed the marketing trends, as evidenced by huge conversion to sales. Facebook, for instance, is a very powerful platform where people from all walks of life around the globe meet, and which business owners take advantage of in order to promote.

There are so many countless benefits from using social media platforms in the realm of business and self-promotion. I can go on and on, but the main idea is still exposure in an unlimited range of audience, just because almost everyone spends most of their day on social media.

Offline vs. Online

It was in the early 1980s when the Internet had been first used by a number of companies and government agencies globally. And through a series of continuous virtual experiments conducted by geniuses and experts to fully endorse the so-called World Wide Web (WWW), it was proven to be a huge success, not only in every office space but in every home using a computer.

The technological changes were rapid enough that in a matter of several short clicks, everything you need to know will be provided to you online. Google it, as we say!

This trend confirmed to be extremely profitable for businesses where various tasks were being outsourced or contracted, which then marked the birth of online jobs and work-from-home opportunities.

This was exactly the reason why I took advantage of this trend. Work can be performed not just in a corporate office space but anywhere, and more so when you're enjoying the laptop lifestyle!

There are lots of online apps (short for applications) that are widely used these days by business owners, for more accurate and efficient results. However, not everyone, myself included, is tech-savvy to use them. Generations X, Y, and Z have well-adapted to these tools. Examples of this are Evernote, Trello, and Google Hangouts.

I will discuss *offline* first. Despite the digital era, there are still quite a good number of businesses that use the traditional way of marketing themselves.

Print advertisements, such as billboards, flyers, and newspaper print ads, are the best examples.

Business experts believe that these traditional methods have high success and conversion rates, and are proven to still work very effectively even until today, the digital age. They also believe that completely replacing the traditional marketing with the latest marketing techniques can be dangerous.

I can personally support this claim because I still use the direct mail method, whereby I write my business proposals to my clients on my business letterhead and mail them directly to their respective office addresses. I find this still effective in increasing my client base, especially that they can appreciate the effort from personalizing the letter, which is nicely printed with a touch of professionalism, authentically signed, and current-dated by yours truly.

In addition, as part of my marketing strategy, I express my appreciation to my existing clients by sending them "Thank You" cards that are sent through regular mail via the post office.

This type of strategy creates more intimate business relationships between myself and my clients, as if they are the only existing client I have. Just because I have a system put in place, I can easily produce bulk letters efficiently, yet personalized for each one of them.

The other known forms of traditional advertising include TV ads in the form of commercials, as well as radio spots that promote a brand, product, or service. These forms are often used by big companies, like the automotive industry and insurance companies, as well as for branded products and services, big events for celebrities and icons, infomercials, and a lot more.

And now, let's discuss *online*. So, let's get social!

I'm convinced that offline marketing strategy still works. However, massive exposure to the global market can be better. And this is made possible these days by our online presence through the use of the newer marketing strategy, through different social media platforms such as Facebook, Instagram, Twitter, and YouTube, etc.

In a typical brick-and-mortar store, customers come and buy products. The same is true for an online store: customers visit your store and buy.

So, what's the difference between the two?

The first type of store has a limited number of buyers. The most likely customers to go and visit that store are those who live in the area, unless it's a highly specialized store that carries a specific and unique item that no other store carries. Unlike the online store, where you can go virtually to the store, no matter where you are on the globe, by visiting the website, and browse the items and pay online. Without having to leave your house or wherever you are, a transaction can get done in a matter of only several short clicks. And the best part is that your items are delivered right to your doorstep.

Let me tell you a sad but true story.

At the time of this writing, Toys R Us, the iconic toy retailer, widely located in the United States and North America, shuts down its 735 stores in the United States, putting roughly 30,000 employees out of their jobs. And it's still yet to be seen how the stores in Canada will evolve.

According to a report, it was alleged that Toys R Us did not fully embrace the online marketing strategy that was once offered to its management by advertisers some years ago. Although I cannot be sure about it, it may be possible that there was a lack of their online presence in order to sustain the business. They may be present online but not fully maximized, which could have contributed to the demise of their brick-and-mortar business.

It was also told that they were not able to explore marketing strategies, allowing Amazon and Walmart to dominate and take the majority's market share.

In my opinion, it would be very ideal to have both offline and online presence, and to integrate them to improve your business's ROI.

There's this marketing rule, called *Rule of 7,* indicating that consumers need to be exposed to a certain message seven times on average before deciding to make a purchase. And I believe that integrating offline and online marketing strategies increases the probability of converting to a sale.

The use of a professionally made website can bring so much exposure to your brand and to your business.

It is fair to say, to win your game, you have to know the rules first. And in our present age, digital rules!

Play digital.

Network and Mastermind Meet-ups

I have also mentioned that I am part of different network groups for my businesses. Most of these groups are paid groups, meaning I pay for my subscription and membership.

Why is it important?

In my real estate investing business, especially in Canada, there are so many pertinent must-knows that investors should pay attention to, such as by-laws, rights and obligations between landlords and tenants, etc. Seasoned investors are keen to these kinds of things. Being connected to successful people in a certain field that you chose is a smart way to succeed in a shorter period of time.

Yes, I know. There's no such thing as a shortcut to success. And I hear you.

That's true.

One of my mentors, Bro. Bo Sanchez, of the Truly Rich Club, said, *"The smarter way to succeed is to learn from other people's mistakes."* Now, it makes sense, right?

Every network group is unique. I have a network of people for my online business as well. They teach how Facebook ads work, how to effectively create a post on social media to arrive at a higher conversion rate, what is appropriate to post, and when to post, etc.

I know you may feel uncomfortable paying for memberships at the outset, especially when funds are not available. You may try to find free network groups initially. However, may I warn you to be very cautious when associating yourself with random people, as you may not be able to spot scammers—not every person you'll meet in network groups has the purest intention to help you. Been there, done that.

Another form of affiliation that you may want to look into is the meet-up groups. You can find them all online. Search according to your business or area of expertise. Because almost everything is done online, joining mastermind groups can be as easy as counting 1-2-3.

Be Visible All You Can

I could remember being offered an online business opportunity in the past. I was directed to its website. It was pretty enticing. However, there was a problem. I couldn't find the founder. What a huge red flag!

I'm convinced that people buy your products or avail your services not because they are actually good but rather because of you. They buy you because they trust and like you! But how you can gain trust and be liked when customers don't even have a clue that you exist.

At least providing your contact information gives your customers that sense of trust to build a business relationship.

When you're well-branded, others may already know you upon hearing your company name or your proper name as your brand. But what if you're still unknown?

Be visible all you can, both offline and online. Have that courage to show your nice face on your website, at the *About Us* section, in your calling cards, flyers, and other marketing materials. If putting your face becomes unnecessary, at least put your business address and phone numbers so that customers can reach you at any time.

Chapter 7
You're Not a Superhero

Stop Calling Me One

A superhero is called as such because he/she possesses superhuman and special strengths to do good deeds and help other people in dire need.

Forgive me here for a second, as I wanted to be frank and straight to the point just for a bit.

I don't know you personally, but what I do know is you're not a superhero. I get it. You want to help others. And I do, too.

I also know that you're hardworking, responsible, organized, brave, and super strong. But still, neither you nor I am close to being compared to one.

What I'm trying to say here is you can only do so much.

I'm guilty of this; I promise! Since I wanted to save money from paying another person (s) to do some stuff for me while I do another task on the side related to my business, it only did more harm rather than good.

The reality is that multi-tasking is not really a good idea. Okay, okay. Maybe, just maybe, sometimes it works.

Here's the truth.

Starting several things all at the same time will almost always *not* deliver the best results you can expect. And as part of my learning curve, I try to do things one at a time, according to priorities and deadlines.

Because I've accepted the fact that...

I CAN'T DO IT ALL.

I Can't Do It and You Can't, Too!

When I totally gave in to the idea of delegating tasks, I started to see favorable productivity in my business and in my personal life.

Doing just one business from home and running your household can already be exhausting. How much more exhausting will it be when there are two, three, four, or more businesses that you have to take care of?

I have a confession to make. Aside from being the old-school type, I have these traits of being obsessed with getting things perfectly organized, seeking attention to details, inclining to be a perfectionist at times, and having the tendency to re-do the work done by others due to unmet standards I set, etc.

I would always feel paranoid.

But I already accepted the fact that "I can't. I just can't do it all." My body and mind (and also spirit) can only take so much workload and stress.

This is what I believe now. Although I know that every person is different—different in a sense that your pain threshold may be higher than mine or you're likely to tolerate some things that I don't—we can only be in unison when overwhelm due to overwork strikes. You surely don't like it, do you? I don't!

So, what did I do?

Continue reading...

The Art of Delegation

Are you a control freak? I'm also guilty of that because I tend to be exactly like one most of the time, especially when it comes to work. But I do realize that nobody can be successful on his own. Success is the end result of a collaboration of efforts exhibited among teammates.

Although I may have started my online business from home as a one-man show, whereby I tried to do things on my own initially, the time came when I had to distribute the tasks so that I could be more effective in creating more productive or result-producing activities, or I should say money-making activities.

As an affiliate marketer, checking e-mails already takes a big chunk of my day because of my responsibility to respond to inquiries, product fulfillment questions, delivery, payments, support, etc.

So, who can do this type of work for me then?

Did I not mention hiring a VA (Virtual Assistant)?

I've hired and used different VAs in my online businesses. They've helped me in a wide range of clerical tasks.

What's so good about being your own boss is that you can set your own rules, and set your pay structure, and the best part...You can choose whoever you want to work with!

The best places to find reliable VAs are:

- Direct referral from family and friends
- Freelancer.com
- Upwork.com
- Fiverr.com
- Virtualemployee.com

A simple task can be priced initially at $5.00, and can then vary, depending on the scope of work. You may also choose to hire them either on a project basis or on contracts (months to years).

A VA can also do logo designs and calling cards for your websites, to name a few.

Tim Ferriss, the author of *The 4-Hour Workweek* book, which truly inspired me to delegate work, shared in his book that he didn't have regular employees for his businesses but instead hired VAs, whose jobs ranged from checking e-mails to setting his appointments and meetings remotely.

It is very beneficial for business owners due to smaller overhead cost for manpower.

Having a virtual team is really worth considering. By doing so, you are indeed buying time and convenience, which is far more important than exhaustion from feeling over fatigued and stressed due to work overload.

He, in fact, endorsed this very important acronym for his *Lifestyle Design in Action,* called D.E.A.L. (D for Definition, E for Elimination, A for Automation, and L for Liberation).

I'm now enjoying delegating work, as I have more opportunity to attend to things that matter, while making money.

The Ugliest Thing Ever

Being in the know is different from wanting to know all. Aspiring to be the *Jack-of-all-trades, master of none,* can be disastrous in any given endeavor.

I've learned that successful people are only experts in one field, although there may be a few who are also very good in more than one. But these are hybrid species.

It's good to know a lot, but it's horrible to attend to multiple things at the same time, as it can greatly affect quality and quantity of your desired results.

Remember, *you're not a superhero; neither am I.*

The Missing Link

Let's assume you've decided to do business (es), either part-time or full-time. It's good that you have goals to reach and a follow-through from your initial steps. But do you know that it's not really a good idea to get started just for the sake of getting started?

Hold on a second and pause. Look for that missing piece of the puzzle: FOCUS.

I have previously stated that doing multiple things at a time can really, really, really be disastrous, unless you're the super-duper hybrid type.

So, why focus?

When I quit my job, almost two years ago, and decided to stay at home and work from home to run several businesses that create passive income streams, I put my very specific timeline. However, while that timeline was not there yet, I focused on positioning myself in areas to support my major shift.

I focused on getting started with one first, mastering the business, establishing a system in place, and delegating the majority of the work. And then, when everything was already smoothly running, I decided to create another income stream that would basically create the same system and model, such that my goal of not having to be there all the time, thus creating passive income, is met. I was able to create multiple income streams because of focusing first in one area, then to the next, and then again to the next, and so forth.

And here's the thing.

Exploring two or more different things at a time will only leave you exhausted and feeling like you are juggling loads of balls all over the place but not accomplishing anything, because this may end up with one or two, or even 100, balls dropping all at the same time, leaving you frustrated and dissatisfied.

If I may say it again, FOCUS on one thing first. Once you're ready to jump to the next, then that's the time to move on and make money on the next, and the next, then the next, and so forth…Because the beauty in focusing on that one thing will certainly bring extraordinary results, and you may say, "It's good. I'll do it again."

Follow this:

Focus to action. Rinse and repeat. Focus to action. Rinse and repeat. Focus to action. Rinse and repeat…And again and again.

And after determining what you should focus on, the next question would be how to do it.

Here's my list that helped me a lot to succeed:

- Write down specific goals.
- Break down those goals according to their timelines (e.g., yearly, monthly, weekly, or daily).
- Schedule your entertainment.
- Take breaks, as necessary, to prevent exhaustion and fatigue.
- Pay attention to yourself and your goals only.
- Rest your mind and body when needed.
- Don't overdo things.
- Calm down.
- Pray.

Chapter 8
From Coming Soon to Now Showing

It's Like a Movie

Four years in the making. It really sounded like a film production in the entertainment industry. There has to be a timeline for a successful movie launch, from script-writing to the actual release of the motion picture, to the viewing public.

I've had my own version of this process, just like in filmmaking, from planning to the actual release of my resignation letter to my manager at my corporate job.

It was a Wednesday morning, at around 10:00 a.m., on June 15, 2016, when I went to meet my manager in her office to tender my resignation, with my actual last day at work on August 15, 2016.

I had a very heavy heart, but I had decided to do that one thing I'd been waiting for in that span of four long years. I loved my job: compensation, benefits, colleagues, environment, and everything about it. Hands down.

I remember this line from Walt Disney: *"The way to get started is to quit talking and begin doing."*

Yes, I literally quit my job, but I also started to do something to make things happen for me, or I'd be stuck to where I was.

Then came August 15, 2016, my last day at work, and I had mixed emotions—excited and scared—excited to fulfill my dream but scared of the unknown.

I did it afraid.

"This is it," I said. I savored the moment.

And so, what now? Here's what I did.

The Big Shift

I was gainfully employed from 1997 to 2016, almost 12 years of which I had worked for a government hospital in downtown Toronto.

On August 16, 2016, as an official stay-at-home mom, I was literally self-employed and slowly transitioned to becoming a business owner. And in the process, while income streams have allowed me to save and invest in profitable avenues, I became an investor and continue to be one.

Don't feel bad about being employed. In fact, I would recommend that you become an employee first because being one provides:

- Financial sustainability due to guaranteed income, for bill payments, basic needs, and covering your household expenses.
- Free access to career and self-development workshops as part of the company's long-term goals to meet the business's competency from their workforce.
- Work experience that you can add to your Curriculum Vitae or work profile.
- Specific skill set (s) that can be applied either in career advancement or to your own business.
- Access to different options, and being able to test the water without having to take the full plunge.
- Realization to discover your passion and interest upon exposure to the real job.
- A more in-depth and realistic experience, having felt both the joys and sentiments of a real employee.
- New perspective and ideas from employer such as hiring and recruitment process, day-to-day operations, etc.
- Improved communication and social skills in order to gain experience in working with people, both colleagues and customers.
- More access to a network of people who can be your source of references in the future.

There are a lot more advantages than these, but I just want to stress the very basic benefits from being employed at the first stages of your working life before you can transition to something later on.

You can probably tell that I've really enjoyed working as an employee, by the number of years I've spent in the corporate world. However, I left because I believed that there's more for me to do—not just for myself but for others, for the ones I love, which led to my BIG SHIFT.

To dream is free, but the hustle is sold separately.

Humans are naturally dreamers. The only difference is in the action that one takes; some just fantasize and don't do anything about it. Subsequently, dreams just cling in the horizon, untouched, unrealized.

"Some people want it to happen, some people wish it would happen, and others make it happen." – Michael Jordan

In other words, one is an action-taker while the other is just a dreamer.

Which one are you?

You have to know this: there's no right or wrong with regard to the size of your dreams. But if you can, dream BIG! What's wrong, I believe, is when one doesn't start that decision to fulfill it. Slow, fast...it doesn't matter. Just keep moving.

The only thing that will prevent you from fulfilling that one dream is your limiting belief.

You may recall in the beginning of this book that I wrote about getting started. It's like building a house from the ground up. The very main foundation should be strong enough to hold the other components. And that foundation is YOU.

Visualize the bigger picture waiting for you. And be inspired. Never stop. Take one step at a time.

"Dream big. Start small. But most of all, start." – Simon Sinek

Goodbye Commute, Hello Telecommute

I've already mentioned about this very important date: August 16, 2016, my first day being officially a stay-at-home mom. It felt somewhat strange, though. I used to wake up at 5:30 in the morning, every single day, Monday to Friday, for almost 12 years to get ready for work. During the weekends, I would set my alarm clock for 6:30 in the morning to start my mommy duties (too numerous to list them all, seriously), and my list goes on.

August 16, 2016 was my official big shift from commuting to go to my 9-to-5 job in the corporate setting, to telecommute in the comfort of my home, performing work tasks for my businesses with my laptop.

Being Good at What You Love

I love taking care of my family, and it's a fact. And because I'm home-based now, I also have the opportunity to focus on doing what I really love: businesses. When I decide to be very good at what I love doing on the side, it now becomes passion and not work.

It may seem obvious that my passion is strong enough—that's why I wrote this book.

I'm passionate about creating home-based multiple income streams, and share to every mom in the world that there's a choice indeed. I used to feel the same sentiments with fellow mothers, how heart-breaking it could be to leave the family, especially the children, for work.

I've discovered in my journey that there's always a solution to a problem. Did I not previously stress the importance of FOCUS?

Also, identifying your emotional WHY will create that drive in you to reach your goals. And once it's determined, you'll surely find every way to be good—really good—at what you love.

My Greatest Influencers

I believe that we tend to become like the persons who we look up to and pattern ourselves with their beliefs, advocacy, teachings, and practices.

I have three individuals who influenced me so much that I follow and, if not exactly the same, become a little bit like them.

I have mentioned about Bro. Bo Sanchez several times in this book previously, whom I met through the Truly Rich Club (TRC), back in 2010. It is a club that teaches how to be abundant in all areas of a person's wellbeing (not only spiritually but most especially financially). He is one of the sought-after public speakers and authors in the Philippines. He delivers his motivational and inspirational talks about relationships with God and others, self-development, and finances, to name a few.

Robert Kiyosaki is an American businessman, a well-known financial literacy activist and speaker, and an author of the very famous *Rich Dad Poor Dad,* a financial book he wrote, which is considered to be the number one personal finance book of all time. This book challenged and changed the way millions upon millions of people all over the world thought about money, and I am one of them.

If you haven't read that book, I encourage you to do so.

He then wrote another book, called *Rich Dad's Cash Flow Quadrant,* which explains the four different types of people who make up the world of business. You may have already seen and known about this, but for the sake of our discussion, let me illustrate the diagram on the next page:

The Cash Flow Quadrant

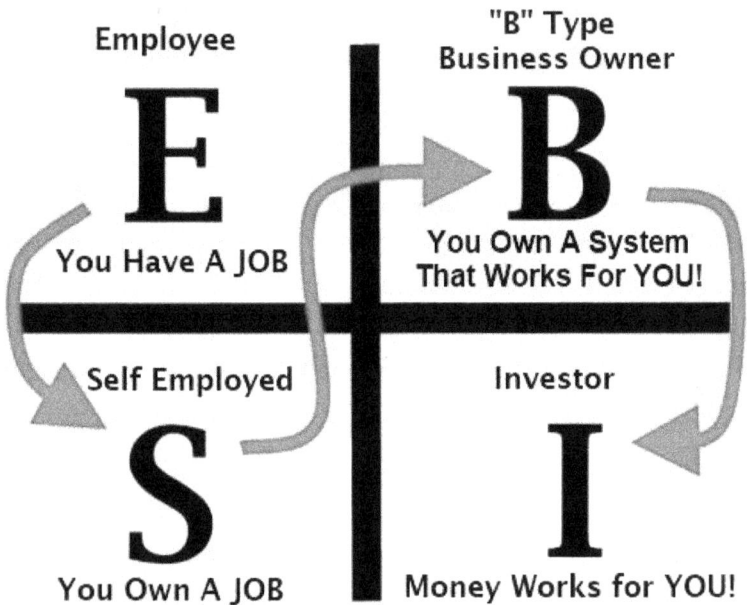

Figure 1.0   Photo Credit: Google

Look closely at Figure 1.0 (above) – The Cash Flow Quadrant.

You'd notice that there are two columns, left and right, with four quadrants altogether that also represent two income types: Active and Passive Income.

On the left, you'll see an E (Employee) and S (Self-Employed) – Active. While on the right, B (Business Owner) and I (Investor) – Passive.

Active income source requires your physical presence to earn money while passive does not. In other words, the primary requires you to trade your time for money, e.g., employee, while the latter indicates you earning income even in your absence.

This Cash Flow Quadrant changed me a whole lot, which gave me the inclination to be at the right side of the quadrant.

Last but not least, I have become the person that I am now because of my own mother, my Nanay Yolly. I know I wouldn't be able to match her beautiful traits as a very hands-on mom and wife, but I followed her footsteps somehow by prioritizing family first above everything else.

She dedicated her whole life in serving my father and everyone in our family. She never stopped offering herself to serve us, even when I have family and children of my own. She was so selfless to put herself last all the time. I admire my mom so much. I'd always wanted to be like her, and subconsciously, in the process, I realized that I followed her footsteps all this time. Thus, I'm now a certified stay-at-home mom, just like her. She also taught me how to be good at handling finances, which I'm able to apply in my personal and family affairs. A big part of me obviously came from her.

Innovate to Scale Up

When I initially started my first home-based business, Transcription, I was very happy with the way it turned out because I was able to clearly define and establish a system for more efficient and effective operations of the business.

But I know that there could be more to that to maximize my income potential through INNOVATION.

I wrote down the characteristics of my business model and examined the different angles, such that I could innovate and scale up to serve more clients, as well as provide more services that are related to my niche.

Here's my list on how to improve your business for innovation, and to maximize its income potential:

- Take random surveys either online or offline.
- Identify a particular problem and look for a solution to that problem.
- Observe your customers' behaviors.
- Ask for comments or feedback about your products or services.
- Run a contest.
- Watch and observe your competition.
- Adapt to the new technological advancement.
- Split test with trial and error.
- Hire an expert for his/her opinion, if at all possible.
- Evolve and explore.
- Be on top of your game.
- Consider bringing your business on a global scale.

Chapter 9
Queen of My Home-Based Business

I assume that by now you have so many things going on in your head with regard to which business start-ups you'd like yourself to get into.

And you may be conditioned by now, as I've initially given you a comprehensive insight about what to expect, as well as about personal preparedness, what a home-work setting should look like, and how your role can be as effective and productive as you possibly can, etc.

I will be discussing, one by one, my home-based businesses.

Transcription

I'm a Medical Laboratory Technologist by profession, and a graduate of Bachelor of Science in Medical Technology, in 1996. I took this four-year course to prepare for medical school, as I wanted to become a medical doctor.

I took and passed my licensure examination for the said degree, in the same year. I never liked the idea of having time wasted; so, while preparing myself for medical school, I looked for a job. I chanced upon a job posting that caught my interest: *Looking for Medical Transcriptionists,* as per the newspaper ad, in February of 1997.

I got hired and enjoyed the job. As a result, I dropped the idea of going to medical school.

Fast forward: I got married, had kids, and migrated to Canada in 2006. I successfully landed a full-time job at St. Michael's Hospital, in downtown Toronto, as a medical transcriptionist. Around the same time, I had been offered an independent contractor (IC) contract from the United States, which I could do from home, also as a medical transcriptionist.

My medical transcription experience improved year after year through massive exposures to different types of clients and medical cases around the globe. And I really loved it. With my own initiatives, I also endeavored to improve myself even more by attending conferences, reading books, and utilizing other helpful tools online and offline to be the expert that I am now.

I capitalized on this experience by looking for more opportunities that gave me even more credibility, and enhanced my skill set.

I did some transcription projects from different affiliations and specialties that scaled up my client base.

Then, a door of big opportunities came sometime between February and March of 2014, when I was afforded to do multi-specialty transcription services for different companies in Canada.

This gave birth to my transcription company, Trans-ACTS & Communications, by which the name was derived from a Bible verse:

"In everything I did, I showed you that by this kind of hard work we must help the weak, remembering the words the Lord Jesus himself said: 'It's more blessed to give than to receive.'" (Acts 20:35)

I ran the business very well with a system put in place, from receiving voice files through my exclusive database to delivering the transcribed reports to the respective recipients.

I scaled up my transcription business by creating other services related to that as a one-stop shop company to serve more clients.

Here's my list of other services I offer:

- Content and Article Writing
- Editing and Proofreading
- Web Design and Maintenance
- Transcription Coaching for Start-Ups
- Remote Clerical Work Services

I also innovated and use my transcription business platform to sell and distribute transcription equipment and office supplies to retailers and wholesalers around the globe. The common ones, but not limited to, include:

- Transcription headsets

- Hand-held devices for recording voice files
- Foot pedals
- Transcription software
- Microphones
- Office supplies

And a whole lot more.

Online and Affiliate Marketing

The next home-based business that I'm so delighted to share with you, as I also generate an unlimited income at any time of the day, 24/7: online and affiliate marketing.

Online marketing is a form of advertising using the internet; that's why it's called as such. It involves different strategies that are appealing to your target market, which can eventually convert or translate into sales. It becomes increasingly important to small businesses of all types. In the past, some business owners thought that because their business was only local, online presence was not needed. What also is equally important as its online presence is its good online reputation. Online reviews also matter. Just one unhappy customer can negatively impact a business reputation, as the news can spread so easily, and as fast as lightning.

Past the Industrial Age, we are now in the Information Age, also known as the Digital or Computer Age.

This present age that we are currently in has brought about changes in the way of marketing or selling products and services to customers through the use of the internet in digital form. Innovations continue to happen, day in and day out, to effectively and efficiently communicate with the world in real time. Changes are implemented consistently due to the way customers behave. In the past, small players in a particular niche couldn't compete with the big ones due to capitalization. But it isn't the case at this time. Everyone, big or small, has the same advantage because of the medium everyone uses: digital or online marketing.

You may have visited a blog site in the past and read its contents. You've probably seen advertisements on the page while you're on that site. The ads are being placed on a page to generate income for the owner of the blog site. Pay-per-click (PPC) advertising is a way to earn income when that ad is clicked. In essence, the blog site is used to host a particular advertisement by a business owner as his/her way to make his products or services known to a particular target market or audience, especially when the blog owner has a significant number of followers and audience.

As of this writing, I'm building my own online course for medical transcription because I truly understand the importance of digital marketing and its power to continuously reach thousands upon thousands of customers in no time, globally.

I've come to realize, although I do coaching for transcription business start-ups, that we only have 24 hours in a day and 7 days in a week. From creating my own *evergreen* online course, I'll be able to help a lot more aspiring transcriptionists in the world.

There are other different types of digital marketing. I will only enumerate the common types for the sake of our discussion, but I will not discuss them in detail. Please feel free to find out more information online.

- SEO (Search Engine Optimization)
- E-mail Marketing
- Social Media Marketing
- Content Marketing
- Video Marketing

I'm also earning passive income through affiliate marketing.

I have several products and services for which I get paid through earned commissions by the owner as a direct referrer.

This is one of the most common ways to get started and earn as soon as possible, if an initial investment to capitalize is a concern. This income stream is very popular in that you're all ready to get started and earn income as early as day one, without having to create your own products to sell or services to promote. When an affiliate marketer is provided with his/her unique affiliate link by the owner, you can start to promote it using different social media platforms, such as Facebook, and earn commissions up to a certain percentage.

The good thing about online and affiliate marketing is that you're not limited to just having one or two. You can have as many affiliate links from different sources as you want.

Although I do understand that the main focus is for extra income, there are two suggestions you may want to consider when getting started:

- Always think about your customers' needs first before your own. Ask this question, "Will it really serve the customers well if they buy it?"
- Let your affiliate programs go in line with your core values and beliefs. Be selective with what you promote.

Portfolio Investment

I also earn passive income through this avenue. But before I delve deeper, let me define some terms for your better understanding.

First, what is a portfolio?

According to thesaurus.com, a portfolio is a flat case for transporting papers. Merriam-Webster defines it as a hinged cover or flexible cases for carrying lose papers, pictures, or pamphlets.

On the investment side of things, it is a collection of investments that can be owned by an individual or an institution.

What types of investments can be in a portfolio?

According to Investopedia, it can span a wide range of asset classes, mainly paper assets that include securities such as stocks, bonds, mutual funds, money market funds, exchange traded funds, stocks, etc.

Let me take, for instance, the easiest example for you to understand it better: stocks.

Stock shares are only one form of hundreds of paper assets that are available everywhere today.

Do you drink Coke, a product of Coca-Cola?

We all know that Coca-Cola is a very established company and brand worldwide. The majority of today's population must have consumed, if not Coke, one of its products, like Sprite, Minute Maid, and Fanta, to name a few.

Coca-Cola is a company, right? For a company to grow its business operations, it needs to continuously raise money or capital. They issue shares, also known as stocks, through what is called Initial Public Offering, or IPO. The price of every share is set, based on how much the company is estimated to be worth and how many shares are being issued. These shares are traded (buy and sell) on an exchange such as PSE (Philippine Stock Exchange), NYSE (New York Stock Exchange), etc.

In essence, a person or an institution who buys shares or stocks of a company becomes a shareholder of that company, which means that you literally have a *share* of that business. And when you say *shares,* they have a monetary value that can be bought and sold using an exchange, as I have mentioned above.

In addition, being a shareholder also gives you certain rights and benefits, such as the right to vote on company matters, as well as receiving dividend payments, which I will explain further.

How does investing in paper assets, such as stock shares, work?

There are some ways on how to buy stocks, which are easy to follow.

The first one is to open an online account, through a broker, where you can deposit cash to buy your shares or stocks. Since it's usually done online, you can access it at any time and do the buy and sell inside your account. Your broker can execute your transaction on your behalf.

As I have also mentioned, paper assets include a whole lot more of investments. However, I personally prefer stocks for three reasons:

- It is easier to understand.
- It doesn't require much of my time.
- There is income flexibility.

You know that I'm a mom to my four wonderful kids. And time is really important for me. I'd like to leverage this very important resource of time. Sometimes it doesn't make sense to stay on a course that's complicated. Stocks are a paper asset that I find the easiest to understand and more flexible in terms of earning money.

Here's how I earn money from my portfolio investment:

- Price per share appreciation
- Dividends

Let's take again, for example, Coca-Cola.

Assuming I bought 100 shares of Coca-Cola, at $5.00 per share, back in 2010. My initial investment was $500. By 2018, the cost per share was $8.00. Technically, if I'd sell my 100 shares today, it would be $800 (minus the stockbrokerage's commission and other fees). Over time, a price per share may appreciate or go up in value.

Caveat: All investments go with a risk and are not always guaranteed. A price per share may not always go up in price, and may pose monetary loss when sold prematurely.

Investing in companies that pay dividends, on the other hand, is also very profitable for a shareholder because not all companies do this. When a company is doing well, it distributes a portion of its profits according to what has been decided upon by its board of directors, etc. The most common forms of dividend payments are in cash or stocks (common).

Paper assets are different from regular savings or checking accounts in a financial institution such as a bank.

But you'd probably say, "A savings account can also accumulate interest, right?"

It's true.

In fact, the vast majority of people lean toward putting their hard-earned money in a bank in the form of savings or checking accounts because they're concerned about security, liquidity, and accessibility.

It's also true.

But you have to know first the difference between saving and investing.

Literally, your account in the bank is just purely saving. While buying stocks or shares is a form of investing.

There are differences between them.

And people chose one over the other because of several reasons:

- Fear
- Lack of knowledge with regard to how money works
- Resources
- Other factors such as misinformation

Of course, I cannot be against putting money in the bank to save because I do that as well; I just don't park my money there. I invest. I would just use a portion to pay bills, or for emergencies, etc. And the extra money that I earn from the multiple income streams (which is the reason why I'm teaching you also to do the same) is being invested for the long term.

Investing in paper assets is also not recommended for short-term goals. Ideally, a minimum of 7 to 10 years should be the goal to maximize the income potential through price appreciation and dividends that I mentioned above.

I have fallen in love with investing in paper assets because it literally makes me more money, with little-to-no time required on a daily basis.

Actively working to earn money is good. But there's even better than that. Money can really work hard for you—even while you sleep! And it is made possible by investing in paper assets such as stocks and mutual funds.

Re-Sale and Consignment

I really love this. I also earn money while at home by doing a re-sale and consignment.

How do these work?

To re-sell is simply an act of selling an item(s) again to a new party. These are physical products that can either be brand new or old (refurbished or second-hand items).

Let me start off with old items and where to get them.

If you're a mom, you don't have to look far. Your best place to get started is your closet.

As a mom to my four children, although we've enjoyed hand-me-down items for some time, we still had accumulated a significant pile of clothes, shoes, books, and toys, to name a few.

It took me a while to figure out the best way to de-clutter.

Yes, I've first considered donating for a good cause. But I still have a mountain of stuff lying around the house. And this is what I did.

I've discovered that old items are hot commodities, especially children's clothes. Now, you can't really imagine how powerful social media platforms are. I was able to find perfect avenues to sell my old and refurbished items very easily.

Aside from re-selling, another means I found, where I can monetize old items, is through consignment.

Consignment is simply the act of giving over to another party custody of any physical goods, and retaining legal ownership of those goods until they are sold through a consignment store.

A consignment store is a place where its owner agrees to sell your items (usually used) at their physical shop for an agreed price.

It initially requires time to do this because you want to make sure that the items you're actually selling are still in excellent condition so that you can maximize profits. This also requires a little bit of creativity and good selling skills. It has now become a little bit faster these days because transactions are usually done online.

Items that can be re-sold and consigned can be anything from used household items, such as kitchenware, to lawnmower and garden tools, etc.

Other places where you can find nice items to re-sell are thrift stores.

A friend of mine makes a living just by selling used books on eBay and Amazon, for a very good profit. It came to a point where it already replaced her income to afford her to resign from her full-time job, and run her online store, while taking care of her three children. She would go to every thrift store she could to find very good deals to re-sell, post online, and convert to money in no time.

Just because selling hasn't been as hard as it used to be, it is a matter of finding hot items, even used, to sell.

Apart from old and refurbished items, I also found a very profitable way to earn double, and even more, by selling brand-new items at discounted prices, which I'd buy wholesale.

Best examples of these are designer bags and branded sports shoes. They have given me a profitable income from home as well. As I increased my income streams, I'd invest in resalable items that I knew would sell in a shorter period of time. I also help other moms I personally know, by selling my new items through consignment.

My re-sellers earn in two ways: markup and profit-sharing.

Last but not least, the items that I find very profitable to re-sell and consign are those that I'd previously mentioned in Chapter 9: my transcription equipment and office supplies.

Because I know my target market, any aspiring transcriptionist will definitely need equipment to get started. I was able to directly get these items from huge manufacturers and distribute them to my re-sellers and consignees.

This type of business requires me to invest a significant amount of money upfront.

The idea here is to find something in your existing business that you can also sell to your target market or customers. New or old, they are both good stuff to sell.

Now, you ask me, "How do I find my customers for the items that I will sell?"

Good question.

I've also mentioned that selling is easier these days than it used to be. We have very useful means online, in that a matter of a few clicks, you'll be able to reach your target market.

Social media platforms, specifically Facebook, are very useful. Because not only is Facebook used worldwide, it is very versatile in its features, which can provide that bridge between buyers and sellers to fulfill a transaction being done online.

Paid Facebook ads also play a very important role in getting your products known to the public, which can quickly convert to a sale due to high probability of reaching your target market. Either paid or free, using at least one social media platform, such as Facebook, Twitter, and Instagram, etc., to name a few, is a must.

You may also want to create your own website to market your products to sell.

Anything is possible these days, so don't fret.

Real Estate Investing

I've intentionally written this as the second to the last item because it requires more study and familiarity in the beginning, as well as continuous learning to succeed as an investor. However, I'm hopeful that you'll be able to learn something from the tips and ideas I am going to share with you through our own journey, such that you, too, can get started with real estate investing.

I grew up as a certified NPA (No Permanent Address). We would re-locate from one place to another, which was several times in a given year.

Was it hard? It surely was.

Growing up, I had this goal of preventing my children from experiencing the same. First thing I had put in my mind was to have a permanent place to live, which we fortunately did back in 2007, when we purchased our first home.

It was in 2010 that we joined the Truly Rich Club, which changed our mindset and perspective about money. As part of the overhaul, we were so fired up that it led us to invest in real estate, in Canada. We bought our first rental property in 2011.

We had initially thought that it was as simple as buying an investment property to rent out, and then we could rest and collect money from the monthly rent. However, we lost a lot of money in the process, through unpaid rents and destroyed property, let alone the stress and sleepless nights this whole experience gave us. This served as a huge tuition fee, which then led us to seeking mentors and network groups for Real Estate Investing in Canada. We joined Real Estate Investment Network (REIN).

We were so pumped to buy our second property, which we again successfully accomplished.

How did we do that?

Our primary residence had accumulated equity from our mortgage pay-down and property value appreciation, which we accessed to serve as the downpayment for our second rental property. Because of our mentors' guidance, as well as our fellow real estate investors' help in our network, we were able to buy another rental property, which, at the time of this writing, earns very well with good tenants from day one.

Because we realized that real estate investing is a very lucrative business, we decided to go to the next level. A few months ago, we had shifted to buying a low-rise apartment building. This required us to put a huge downpayment upfront, which again came from the equity we had accumulated from the first and second properties we bought.

If you'd notice, we actually didn't put in a lot of money to have multiplied our rental properties in the process. Although we've had a fair amount of out-of-pocket expenses for closing costs, such as lawyers' fees, insurance, inspection, some minor renovations, etc., we were able to make use of the available equity that we had accumulated over time.

Although it wasn't an easy process, it also wasn't that hard for young investors like us because we sought proper guidance from our mentors and other seasoned investors in our network.

If you're thinking about investing in this asset class, you may want to look into the exact steps we did that may also work for you:

- Build a good credit score. A credit score is the primary number that banks and financial institutions would look for to check an applicant's creditworthiness. In other words, paying debts or loans on time is the first qualification that mortgage providers will look for first in an applicant.

- Proof of income or funds. A downpayment is always required by the lender, and its source needs to be verified at all times. The lender also requires the loan applicant to prove his/her ability to pay the amortizations on a regular basis, and where these funds are coming from. Proof of employment is highly recommended to get considered for a loan.

- Clean criminal background. This is self-explanatory. No company will ever agree to have business with anyone that has a criminal history or legal issues.

From my very own experience, we started off with just one property: our primary residence. We let its equity build on its own by paying our mortgage on time consistently, topping up payments when able, maintaining our good credit scores, and staying in our day jobs for proof of income. It also made it easier for our loan application and approval because we were able to show multiple sources of funds, such as our side hustles and other businesses.

But what if...

You don't have the capacity yet to buy a rental property, or even your primary residence.

Let me give you examples that you may also want to do to get started.

I learned some tips from people I know in the business. And that's the reason why talking to like-minded people will really benefit you in the most unexpected time:

Example 1:

Let's call him Joe. He doesn't own a house. He is just renting his three-bedroom townhouse for $1,500 a month. He's married with a 5-year-old child. His wife is a stay-at-home mom, taking care of their son and the household.

This is what he did.

He rented out his two other bedrooms for $650 each, to students. Because he had no car at that time, he also rented out his parking space for $100 a month. His basement was fully finished and furnished, which also afforded him to rent out for an extra $800 to another set of renters.

So, let's do the math:

- Bedroom 1: $650
- Bedroom 2: $650
- Basement: $800
- Parking: $100
- Total: $2,200

How much was he paying his landlord monthly?

Yes, you're right. He was paying $1,500 a month. But he was earning $2,200 because he leveraged the property by re-renting the available spaces to other renters.

Caveat: To do this, you must have a written agreement between you and your landlord to prevent any forthcoming issues. Verbal agreement isn't enough, as unexpected disputes may arise at some point.

Over the course of several years, he was able to save money for the down payment for his own house and, eventually, bought a second property for rental.

Of course, during the process, he also took care of his credit score, proved his source of income through employment, and never had legal issues.

Example 2:

Emily owns a vacant lot. She didn't know at that time what to do with it until she was approached by a neighbor, named Lily, who owned three cars. Lily rented two parking spaces from Emily, for a fixed amount of $160 monthly for both. The information spread in the village, and everyone in her area with not enough parking spaces also rented Emily's space. She would earn a total of $700 for 10 cars, on a monthly basis, which she saved and used to buy another vacant lot for the same purpose.

You see, there's no excuse to not invest in real estate. It may take a while, but it's a very good source of passive income that can afford you to buy more properties in due time.

Find mentors in your area. Never do it alone without proper guidance. You'll reap the great benefits in the end when you do it properly at the beginning.

I Will Sell You

Yes, you read it right. It's pretty straightforward. I will sell you anything I think you'll need. That salesperson in me sparks when a conversation starts to indicate something. It may not be a physical product, but most of the time I sell my services as I see fit.

One of the best perks of being a mom is you get to know a lot of things and ideas that you can share to others as well, because of your wide experience and skills that all started at home.

Tip: Listen to every person talking to you. You don't know what business opportunity may arise from that conversation. And that can only happen when you start closing your mouth and start listening instead.

Imagine, creating multiple income streams from home is really, really amazing. I can absolutely tell you that my ultimate goal was to create more PASSIVE income from different sources, such that I could literally fulfill my goal of leaving my corporate job to being a stay-at-home mom to serve my family, which I now did after four long years of preparation and planning.

As I become more passionate every day, and be the expert that I am in what I do, I intend to follow *The 4-Hour Workweek,* by Tim Ferriss, in no time, such that I can be physically present to the matters that really, really, really matter to me, and which make me complete and happy: my relationships.

As we almost end, I'd like to share with you my formulas to get me to the point of success that I celebrate every day.

Here you go.

Chapter 10
My Success Formulas

My Belief System

There's this belief system that I planted in myself for success.

In my mind, my heart, and spirit, I always declare and believe that:

- I'm God's child.
- I'm His beautifully made masterpiece.
- I can all do things through Christ who strengthens me (Philippians 4:13).
- There are only two opinions that *should* matter: God's opinion about me and my opinion about myself.
- I can be fruitful and prosperous, and be a blessing to others.

This belief system works very well for me, as I instill in my mindset every day. By training my thoughts regularly, negative vibes are immediately blocked from entering my brain.

These five reminders make a difference in my life, big time.

You may also want to structure your own belief system that will better equip you as you travel in this journey called life.

Winning My Relationships

You may recall the scriptural order of priorities that I wrote above. I will enumerate them again, according to importance: God, spouse, children, parents, extended family, and then the rest of the world.

To grow as a person, it's a requirement to win every healthy relationship as much as possible, be it in your marriage, family, friendships, or even in business. However, not every relationship is worth keeping. Toxic ones that bring your energy down are worth letting go.

Be surrounded by like-minded people who can uplift and help you grow even more as a person.

Invest in good relationships. It will surely bring you somewhere.

At the end of the day, everything is all about relationships—good relationships—as it were for me.

W.E.A.L.T.H.

My success lies in the foundation of my WEALTH. I used them altogether to arrive at my desired destination.

W – Wisdom. Again, from the scriptural order of priorities, seeking God first, and His wisdom, is my best secret for success. You'd recall, in my introduction, that I sought God's approval for me to leave my job, but I never stopped there. Yielding to His will on an ongoing basis makes my journey to be so smooth that I'd think everything is scripted.

E – Education. I've mentioned several times how important it is for success, to seek education through investing in oneself to learn more. Learning affords you to be positioned in a better vantage point. Opportunity oftentimes favors the prepared. Also, looking for mentors in your field of interest is also one of the best ways to succeed. I have mentors, and they guided us so well. Results will speak for themselves.

A – Ability. Believing in your ability to do wonderful things can bring you to the next level of success or even greater than what you expect. Had I believed that a mom like me couldn't have the opportunity to excel in the realm of business, I wouldn't be able to now enjoy the perks of being a serial entrepreneur. I never let anybody's opinion about me steal my goals and dreams. You, too, can make things happen for yourself. Believe that you're able!

L – Love. Being able to do something that you really love is passion. This one main ingredient will never make you feel exhausted or have a sense of burnout. I'm passionate about being a serial mommy entrepreneur because of my one sacred purpose: to serve my family while I serve others through entrepreneurship.

T – Talents. Everyone is born unique. We are all given gifts and talents to use and bless ourselves and the world. However, when these are not used, they fade away. I have my own set of skills and talents that I took advantage of to make this world a better place. Yes, I may not be like Thomas Edison who invented the light bulb, but I know that I've made a difference somewhat in the lives of other people, in my own little ways, by using my talents. Sharing our talents with others is an indication of success.

H – Hunger. Successful people stay hungry, seeking for more opportunities and improvement all the time. I continue to improve and innovate, as I believe there's more. Don't get stuck with where you are. Explore and evolve.

Attitude of Gratitude

That one very powerful habit that I find really helpful in making my life happier and focused, as well as creating better perspective in life, is the Attitude of Gratitude.

Waking up every morning is more than enough reason for me to be thankful. It anchors my positive thoughts and proper mindset in my everyday life, from start to finish. It also improves all my relationships, thus creating a healthier body, mind, and spirit—a very holistic approach.

All things that happen to me regularly, big or small, contribute to the evolution of my wellbeing. Even though I know things can't always go the way I want them, I'm still thankful because they help me grow.

Being thankful also invites that sense of good vibes coming to me, as if the universe connives to bring every favor that my heart so desires, blessing me and the people I love. Be grateful. It's contagious. It's beautiful. It's sacred. Let's always be grateful.

My Prayer for Abundance

To the Most High I pray and these words I ought to say
In love You came to me, and I praise Thee
as you embrace me
I ask for Thy boundless Might to look down upon me
In that I may be truly blessed despite
my flaws and shortcomings.

Cleanse me today, Oh Lord, to be worthy of
Thy loving mercy
Let the Holy Spirit reside in me as I go today
in my life's journey
I now open myself to receive Your abundant gifts
As You hand down your generosity with such power
and great bliss.

You're my strength and my shield
My ever present help in times of every need
Grant Your protection for me and my family
Such that the works of the enemies can't play a curse on me.

As I long for Your abundance, every day is another chance
For this I know You're wonderfully faithful by
Your capable hands
You gave Your life to me and saved my soul completely
Even though I stumble and fall short of Your glory.

I now declare to have received Your abundant blessings
Abundance on finances, good health, and relationships
May I multiply these gifts to love and to serve
You more and others

With all of my strength now and forever.
I thank Thee for Thy goodness and generosity
I'll be ever mindful of the things You've done for me
Because by Your love, power, and light
I'm a complete person and the apple of Your eyes.

*"Let NOT fear stop you from being the best version of
yourself and fulfilling your God-given purpose."*
– Anna Santos

Mommy Means Business

Premier of Ontario
Premier ministre
de l'Ontario

Ontario

Legislative Building
Queen's Park
Toronto, Ontario
M7A 1A1

Édifice de l'Assemblée législative
Queen's Park
Toronto (Ontario)
M7A 1A1

August 14, 2018

Ms. Anna Santos

Dear Ms. Santos:

Thanks very much for the copy of your book, *Mommy Means Business*. It was great to hear from you, and I appreciate your taking the time to share your personal story with me. I was sorry to read about the struggles you experienced following the birth of your fourth child, and commend you for the courage you demonstrated in addressing that challenging situation.

I want to congratulate you on your success in managing both family life and a career. It was good of you to document your experience so that others can find inspiration in your example.

Thanks again for writing and for your kind gift.

Sincerely,

Doug Ford
Premier